Brain Health Mistakes

instafool

Presents

Brain Health Mistakes

10 Top Mistakes to Avoid to Keep Brain Healthy and Prevent Cognitive Impairment

Instafo

instafo

ISBN 979-8-700-38361-5

Printed in the United States of America

First Edition

FOOL'S GUIDE

PROLOGUE:
The Fool Card

"A fool thinks himself to be wise, but a wise man knows himself to be a fool." – **William Shakespeare**

Ready to have your fortune read? Then pick a card...any card. Ah, congratulations! You have selected the **Fool card.** *Don't* *despair!* It is the most powerful one, being the omnipotent wild card as well as the first card in a tarot deck with the number 0, that represents new journey and new solution available with unlimited optimism, unexhausted enthusiasm, and undiscovered opportunities, because to a fool...anything is possible!

Yet, the fool is "nobody's fool" but is *secretly* the wisest of all, able to pull strings in the most dire situations due to a sharp wit, astute acumen, erudite knowledge, diligent resourcefulness, and perceptive observation of the world and what goes on around. Indeed cunning, evasive, and elusive to get ahead without being ensnared by the same established rules others played by, the fool is able to think and see things outside of the box.

With that said, you can learn a lot from the fool through all their intentional and unintentional antics.

Nobody likes to hear the truth. *The truth hurts...but is honest.* Historically, only the fool was sly enough to get away with the most unfavorable truth in the royal court from knowing everything that went on, without getting his own head chopped and served on a king's silver platter for the hidden genius disguised as superficial foolishness. Perhaps a forgivable trickster in this regard, the fool was, nonetheless and above all, a true survival of the fittest and a formidable force to behold.

If you want to possess the great wisdom of the fool in a modern era of instant information, look no further because you have found your tarot calling card: **Instafool**.

Being an Instafool is for those fools who dare question and go up against conventional knowledge, by exploring the polar opposite side of the coin which nobody else is willing do and by exposing the cold-hard truth which nobody else is willing to admit, in order to gain better perspective, bigger picture, and wider spectrum covering all aspects of everything in any area.

While the fool may be a joker, the Instafool is no joke or laughing matter. Being the Instafool is about being a renaissance visionary trailblazing innovative ideas and being an inquisitive intellect uncovering controversial truths and unapologetically and shamelessly willing to educate those truths, even when gaining ridicules from others.

It's better to be an Instafool than be fooled in a world full of so much instant MISinformation. *Know thy truth by knowing thy untruth.* That's the key role of the Instafool.

This now sums up the Instafool and your tarot card reading. What shall you do now is entirely up to you...

Shall you be audacious enough to follow this path of an Instafool?

ANECDOTE:
The Fool Iffy

Meet "Iffy the Fool" of the high king. He's the fool for the royal court's amusement by entertaining them, but more importantly...indirectly educating them with his endless clumsy antics at the expense of his competence and confidence...for all to see what not do and avoid.

Don't be like Iffy the Fool. Be the opposite of him through learning from his mistakes and doing the opposite of what he does.

Whether intentional or unintentional, the wise fool in disguised accidentally becomes the best teacher around.

He shall now be your guide...

F(OOL) ACT AT PLAY:
Neural Circuitry Disconnected

"Wanna keep your brain from turning into mush—and yourself from losing your marbles?"

That may sound flippant, but we are addressing something we've all seen, and some are now experiencing— "brain decline"—the gradual diminishing of our ability to think and communicate clearly. Our brains tend to wear out as we get older, just like everything else in our bodies. We tend to miss this slow deterioration since the process itself may take decades ("You should live so long!"), a very slow change over a long time.

How can you tell? What are some warning signs? Pay attention to these crucial "check engine" lights. This is serious and if they apply to you, address them with your health care provider RIGHT AWAY!

- Are you experiencing sudden "short-term memory loss"? Are you unable to remember what happened a few minutes or a few hours ago? Do you find yourself wondering how you ended up where you are and what you were supposed to do before you got there?

- Are you unable to find the correct words to use? Is your vocabulary disappearing? Do you have trouble pronouncing certain words you have used before? Do you have trouble writing them down?

- Are you having trouble grasping certain words or concepts? Are you unable to describe something familiar? For instance: is a "magazine" only something you read, or is it also the part of a pistol where the bullets are kept?

If you are aware of the development of any of these deficits in your ability to think or communicate, or if those around you begin pointing them out to you ("Gee, Dad, you seem to be having lots more trouble with your words"), then go! See your doctor now! There may be conditions that may require specific medical or surgical attention. *Do not wait!* Get this checked out ASAP!

Okay. Now that we are past the <u>warning signs</u>, it's time to address how to get our brains in better working order, and possibly prevent or delay our brains from degenerating. The good news is—brain health is not rocket science.

We already know that what we do in life has an effect on how our bodies and brains work. And the brain itself is not totally "hard-wired;" it is not "set in concrete." Our brains have the ability to continually work around various problems. This is called "neuroplasticity"— "neuro" refers to brain cells; "plastic" means "moldable."

We will take a look at the <u>things to avoid</u> as well as the <u>actions to take</u> to help maintain our neuroplasticity and keep our brains in the best condition possible. If people follow these recommendations, they will benefit from them in staying as mentally sharp as they can, for as long as they can.

<u>SELF-EVALUATION</u>: Before we begin flexing your neuroplasticity, we start off with a short self-evaluation, to give you an idea of where you are concerning your "cognitive state," and also to help us define what we're talking about. Please answer these questions "Yes" or "No":

1. Do you spend several minutes trying to remember what you are trying to do?
- Yes
- No

2. Do you call someone and then forget what you were just about to tell them?

- Yes
- No

3. Do you hesitate to do something that would make you think harder and longer?

- Yes
- No

4. Do you feel numb after working for too long at night?

- Yes
- No

5. Do you feel like your mental sharpness is declining as you age?

- Yes
- No

(That's an <u>odd number</u> list of questions...so you cannot take refuge in a *break-even tie*!)

- If you answered mostly "Yes," then you will need to apply corrective action—what we will cover upcoming—in order to be able to keep your wits as sharp as possible (maybe even razor-sharpen them a bit).

- If you answered mostly "No," then you are already doing at least some of the right stuff. Don't stop here, proceed on. You might find additional stuff helpful for yourself; you definitely will find something to help someone else.

<u>DISCLAIMER</u>: Just so you know, we will not be talking about specific mental health conditions—such as "schizophrenia" or "bipolar disorder." We are not trying to fix anything like that. We will also not be talking about the consequences of head trauma or things like tumors or infections or strokes. We are trying to slow down or even prevent the gradual loss of our "cognitive abilities"—our ability to think and communicate clearly—as we age. We

are trying to keep our minds sharp and clear for as long as we possibly can. It will take some work, so some changes in your life will be necessary. Remember, if you have any condition that needs a doctor's care, then get a doctor's care. Don't add any activities or make any changes unless your health care provider believes the changes won't hurt you.

MISTAKE #1:
Insufficient Text Processing

Read more. *Lots more.* Reading stimulates the brain, body, and beyond. When we read fiction, we enter into the plot and the minds of the characters. We engage our imagination and visualize the people and their surroundings. If we are reading non-fiction, we are digesting facts and formulating a conclusion. We determine if we agree with the author's position. We puzzle over the ramifications of the author's conclusions. We keep thinking, using our gray matter, not just letting it be an unresponsive sponge.

Of course, reading is not everyone's cup of tea. Sometimes others don't see the value of reading, particularly reading for the sheer enjoyment of it. If we don't want to be thought of as "too clever for our own good by half" because we read for our personal edification, then we should not show off the cool and interesting stuff we are acquiring with those who do not appreciate our enthusiastic pedantry. Our point is that the activity of reading, whatever the words are or whatever the type of material we read, it's the reading itself that is beneficial for us. It helps keep our minds sharp. Reading is empowering—it's FUN-damental. Nobody else needs to know that we are becoming smarter.

Reading books used to be the primary form of education, as well as entertainment. Today we watch TV, stream videos, or spend hours on social media. These newer things can be interesting, but they're not really all that great for us. Why?

- Our brain stays in idle mode because the content itself isn't mentally stimulating; watching something on the screen is generally a passive experience. Our brains aren't "engaged."

- Our eyes bear the brunt of always staring into the artificial light of our phone or tablet or whatever. (But since our focus here is our brain, we'll leave the issue of eye strain for another topic).

We need to avoid a continual passive soaking-up of the monotonous and really dumb stuff that is thrown at us daily on our various devices. We are zombifying our brain; we are letting it rot to the core. Thus, we need to reconnect with good old reading.

REASONS: In an article in the journal Neurology (July 3, 2013), Dr. Robert S. Wilson, Ph.D., of Rush University Medical Center in Chicago concluded that stimulating the brain throughout one's life, particularly by reading, "is important for brain health in old age." The study evaluated 294 older adults for about 6 years before their deaths (at the average age of 89!). The researchers tested cognitive ("thinking") abilities and how well their memories were working. The old folks also filled out questionnaires about how much they read or participated in other mentally stimulating activities in childhood, adolescence, adulthood, and old age. If the person had lots of stimulating mental activity later in life, their brains held up better—they could think and communicate more clearly, and their memory was better (by 32%!) than folks with average mental activity late in life. If a person in the study wasn't very active at all in exercising their mental capacities, their cognitive abilities (communication and memory) declined 48% faster than those in the "average" group. Do the math: if you keep your brain working even as you age your mental abilities decline at a rate 80% slower than if you let yourself turn into a mental couch potato.

<u>BENCHMARK</u>: It's a good idea to develop a love of reading early in life. Read something every day and encourage those around you to read. Generally, it doesn't so much matter what you read, but you can keep your brain stimulated and "hooked on reading" by reading good books, whether fiction or non-fiction. Look for books where the author has come up with a sophisticated plot or has a writing style that appeals to you. Try finding out what you

like to read; follow a particular series; become better informed on a subject that interests you. Even if you are not totally enthralled with reading, read to your children or your grandchildren; volunteer at your local library to read to other people's children.

A little recommendation to consider: a book written by Mortimer Adler: <u>How to Read a Book</u>—it's certainly not the most entertaining book to read, but it gives suggestions on how to read different kinds of literature like fiction, poetry, and non-fiction of various types.

<u>TASK</u>: Start reading more from now on, even just a little. "Baby steps." Read a newspaper every morning while drinking your morning cup of Joe. Start reading novels or short stories in the evening—start with 7 pages to get into the habit, then gradually increase the volume amount you read. Take the time.

MISTAKE #2:
Abandoning Physical Writing

This may sound a bit disconnected from your reality: *don't we already write every day, something? Ahem, I gotta go now and update my social media's status, text my friend, and send that email.* Perhaps, but how much do we actually write—in other words, how much do we *physically* put down on paper? And what do we write about?

It is very easy, nowadays, to not have to jolt anything down at all. *Period.* "Alexa, add spaghetti sauce to the grocery list." "Siri, add my dentist appointment for October 4th at 10:30. Remind me that morning." The "smart technology" does all the work; you no longer have to hunt for a pen and write something down on a paper calendar. *Such convenience, right? Wondering what else are they going to come up with next?* Obviously, things even more amazingly advanced; but therein lies the problem of convenience becoming a clutch, forsaking the usage of our brain to only be collecting neural dusts.

<u>REASONS</u>: Any opportunity to write (with pen or pencil in hand) exercises our fine motor skills. It stimulates areas of the brain that increase our comprehension. Regular writing—like keeping a journal—increases our creativity and deepens our thinking. Do you remember the study by Dr. Wilson of Rush University we cited previously? The researchers also studied their subjects' writing habits. They concluded that, along with reading, we keep our minds sharper when we write stuff down.

<u>BENCHMARK</u>: Get used to writing out a daily schedule or a "to do" list. If you keep a journal, stimulate and work your brain by reflecting and figuring out how to express in words things that bother you; you may even automatically figure out solutions to your current problems. In writing

these things out, you are enhancing your calm; writing becomes a type of emotional and mental therapy.

<u>TASK</u>: Set up a time to write about 15 minutes before bedtime. Think of it as something to help you relax. What to write? Take the first 5 minutes to figure that out, maybe tomorrow's schedule, or prioritize your "to do" list, events of the day, thoughts on the present or future, and so forth. Yes, habits are hard to establish, but "wherein is the joy of an easy task?" You'll see over time that as you develop the habit of writing things down, your mind will feel refreshed and cleared along with your whole body. After all, your mind is your body's control center, and you are its commander sending it commands through thoughts in writing.

MISTAKE #3:
Not Keeping Brian in Shape

"Brain exercises" are any form of activities that make us think and push us to solve problems. We don't need to ponder the answer to the ultimate question of life, the universe, and everything (we can if we desire to, of course). But simple things will suffice, like word puzzles or board games like Monopoly or Scrabble. We can push our minds to work on solutions to simple problems, such as whether or not to buy Park Place in a Monopoly game.

An often-quoted scientist, Dr. Elise Caccappolo, Ph.D., associate professor of Neuropsychology at Columbia University Medical Center in New York (they are doing some interestingly cool stuff with the brain and aging there) recommends exercising the mind throughout life to help maintain a healthy brain even into old age.

REASONS: Now why aren't we in the habit of doing our mental calisthenics and neurological weight training? Well, it is incredibly easy to find dumb-down entertainment. We can stream movies on our cell phones—the big screen becomes the tiny screen. It has become way too easy to just shut off our brain and suck up whatever drivel is put in front of us. In some cases, it's just not "cool" and "trendy" to pursue anything beyond the pop scene. *(Who're we hanging with?)* On the other hand, some of us work so much that we're too tired to pay attention to anything other than sleep when we get home. We can't engage our brain because we're simply too pooped.

BENCHMARK: The tools to exercise our minds are simple; they range from free to cheap, and we can obtain them just about anywhere. We've seen them often and not noticed. Check out the puzzle books—crosswords, sudoku, word-finders, and others—that are pretty much on any magazine or newspaper rack in grocery and department stores. Go to your app stores and download the digital equivalent versions of them. Those things seem like timewasters, but they do help to keep our minds engaged, particularly interacting with words and basic numerical calculations. When we have family or friends to interact with, we can play board games like Scrabble, or work on jigsaw puzzles, or build the Millennium Falcon out of Legos. All of these activities are good for the mind. They certainly fire up the gray matter.

<u>TASK</u>: Start with the simple puzzle books, like crosswords that have the solutions in the back, so you don't lose to frustration—but no peeking! Try 3 different kinds of puzzles and work on one or two puzzles out of each book every day. When you finish one book, get another one but of a different type of puzzle. For apps, a few of our recommendations are Lumosity, Brainwave, and Elevate, with over a hundred more you can choose from aimed at exercising various capabilities of the brain like creative thinking, problem solving, and critical analysis. Don't do

the same thing over and over again, mind you. Stop doing word-finders and build a model of the Eiffel Tower out of Legos. Then switch up the Legos for sudokus. Keep it up. Start now, however old you are. As cliched as this sounds—it is really good for you.

MISTAKE #4:
A Lack of Brain Fuels

It's true: "We are what we eat." That is true of our brains as well. Most of us don't pay attention to our diets with respect to the needs of our brain cells—too much fast food, too much sugar, yet too few fatty acids that can fuel our brains and help our minds stay sharp.

Yes, fatty acids. They come from the fats and oils we eat. We are primarily concerned here with three of them— together called "omega-3 fatty acids." (<u>Caution</u>: Some Big Words Ahead!) Those are *alpha-linolenic acid* (ALA), *docosahexaenoic acid* (DHA), and *eicosapentaenoic acid* (EPA). Since the names are a mouthful, we will use the abbreviations instead (and remember that in this context

"EPA" does not refer to the Environmental Protection Agency).

We all need to eat stuff that contains these fatty acids. According to the National Institutes of Health, certain plant oils such as soybean and canola oils contain ALA. We consume EPA and DHA when we eat fatty fish like sardines, anchovies, mackerel, and salmon. We may have heard our parents tell us that fish is "brain food." They were right.

REASONS: As a teensy bit of biochemistry to start, ALA, DHA, and EPA are important parts of the cell membranes of all the cells in our body. DHA is found in high concentrations in the cells of our retinas (our eyes) and in our brain cells. Omega-3 fatty acids have a bunch of other functions in the body as well. Lots of information can be found on the US National Institutes of Health website at www.nih.gov; once there, search for "omega-3."

<u>BENCHMARK</u>: If you didn't know before, you know it now: fish is one of the important food sources for omega-3 fatty acids. So, eat more fish! No, we don't need to spend all day eating at a sushi bar, although good sushi is incredibly tasty. We don't need to guilt ourselves into ordering anchovies on our pizza (unless we do like anchovies). Alternatively, there are also other foods that help increase our intake of these necessary nutrients:

- Seeds and nuts: chia seeds, flaxseed, and walnuts
- Plant-based oils: flaxseed oil, soybean oil, and canola oil
- Fortified foods: eggs, juice, and dairy products

Here's something a bit off the wall: watch the movie <u>Lorenzo's Oil</u>—Nick Nolte and Susan Sarandon play parents of a child, Lorenzo, who has an infrequently-diagnosed neurologic condition that has no cure. They figure out that the child's brain responds to certain types of vegetable oils which contain the right kinds of fatty acids. The movie is based on true events—check it out.

<u>TASK</u>: Face it, you need to eat more fish! Okay, you don't need to eat it constantly— "let's have fish for every meal"— radical changes like this are almost impossible to do, and they don't help us thoughtfully make important changes in our lifestyles. Look at your diet and figure out how to add in foods with omega-3's. Add nuts to your diet (not, of course, if you are allergic to them); cook with canola oil on occasion. Eat fish instead of red meat once or twice a month to get used to it. Omega-3's are also readily available as supplements, since these same fatty acids are really good for our hearts. Find whatever suits you. *We aren't Instagram foodie snobs here, or are you?*

MISTAKE #5:
The Clutch of Smart Automation

Automation is a tool; we use a lot of it...and we do mean, a lot of it. Most of the time, automation helps us get more done, almost like magic. *What is this sorcery used for?* We definitely prefer not to wash our dirty laundry out by hand if we don't have to. We would rather not stare at a clock the entire time while we're baking bread; we would set a timer (electronic or otherwise).

We have electronic schedulers on our phones that can keep us from missing important to-dos, like getting up in the morning, attending an appointment, eating lunch, taking our medications, and the list goes on. Simply put, we love our little push-button helpers and can't enough of them. The verdict? They won't be going away any time soon, but only become more prominent in every aspect of our lives. That's where our brain begins to get sidelined and suffer.

<u>REASONS</u>: Unsurprisingly, there are undoubtedly problems if we overdo the automation:

- We don't keep our memory capability in check. When the time does come to learn something that requires repetition, we will be caught off guard and feel the rustiness. That is because we don't train our brains to store and retrieve information.

- We don't accustom ourselves to thinking about what we are doing. Our digital assistant tells us what to do and we do it. We become passive in our activities, leading to the steady decline of our ability to do stuff.

- We don't transform our thoughts into actions. If we don't use our fine motor skills (writing, for instance), and if we don't use our gross motor skills (getting up off our backsides to find a book to read, for instance), we lose coordination.

Okay, we may work in an environment that forces us to use these electronic tools, and they are a huge time-saver for many, many things. But we need to think thoroughly about how we live. Are we reading for ourselves, or are we letting the "book" read to us like we are a very young child? Are we using Siri to dictate an email when we should instead sit down and actually write a letter? Are we binge-watching the TV every weekend? We need to engage our minds and bodies both together to keep ourselves healthy and capable of enjoying life. Truly we need to have time to relax, but we should never become lazy!

<u>BENCHMARK</u>: Start limiting the use of automation so that your brain works along *with* the automated tools. Train your brain to coordinate your hands, eyes, and

memory altogether by organizing tasks in writing. Have fun coming up with ways to help you remember those tasks broken down into steps as well. For example, say you are an event organizer. You use Alexa to remind you of an important catering preparation needed for the upcoming week. After you get that reminder, prepare the rest of the event by thinking and writing things down. Take your notebook and list the names of the caterers in blue, their contact information in green, and all the crucial elements needed to be met in red—using custom colorings to facilitate memory.

Another suggestion: watch the Pixar movie <u>WALL-E</u>. Look at what has become of the people due to the level of automation in their lives.

<u>TASK</u>: Find something technical to read, analyze it, and summarize it in your own words, without someone else explaining it to you. Do your own investigative digging for answers to questions without asking Alexa. Write a letter by hand on paper. Plan a project all meticulously thought

out from A to Z: what is it you want to get done? What supplies do you need to buy? What tools will you use? When and where will you do the actual work? How long will it take? Imagine it; think it; do it. Both mind and body benefit.

MISTAKE #6:
Overloading Inputs and Overwhelming Brain

Aren't we all ever-so impressed by those who can do a million things at once? We envy their relentless self-discipline; we stand in awe of their serendipitous talents. *But, sorry to be the one to tell you that Santa Claus and the Easter Bunny aren't real.* It turns out that multitasking is not all that great for us—and may even be detrimental.

REASONS: In a study entitled "Executive Control of Cognitive Processes in Task Switching" (Journal of Experimental Psychology: Human Perception and Performance, 2001) the authors found out that the participants lost a lot of time switching from one task to another and lost more as the tasks became increasingly complex. Productivity was reduced in some cases as high as 40% as opposed to someone doing the same group of tasks one at a time.

A later study entitled "Cognitive Control in Media Multitaskers" (<u>Proceedings of the National Academy of Sciences</u>, September 15, 2009) found that folks that habitually multitasked "performed worse on a test of task-switching ability, likely due to reduced ability to filter out interference from the irrelevant task set." They apparently couldn't get their minds out of the groove they were in when they needed to do something different.

Even computers do only one thing at a time—albeit really, really fast. In the deepest electronic recesses of our computer's thinking, the processor loads an instruction set, then accomplishes that particular task for a specific period of time, then loads a different instruction set, then works on that particular task, and so on, over and over and over. We don't see the "overhead," the time used to "switch gears" between processing a keystroke and moving the mouse pointer on the screen. This is because computers process data too quickly for us to perceive. Who of us is going to miss a few thousand nanoseconds?

BENCHMARK: "But," you say, "multitasking is part of how we live." True. Life is indeed complex: we have to keep stirring the sauce, while in another pot on the stove we're cooking the noodles. And sometimes we have to shut off both the noodles and the sauce and attend to the baby—then it's time to forget what's on the stove—after turning off the heat, that is—and order out some pizza (with anchovies). This is a reasonable way to manage the situation. But we don't do this with everything. We don't sit down to read a novel, then after a page in the first novel switch to another story, then after a page there change to a third book. No, we read one book at a time.

Look at your life and how you do the stuff you do: can you get more done by doing your tasks *sequentially* instead of *simultaneously*? Can you get all your work done by doing one thing at a time? It's one thing to feel overloaded but it's another to purposefully overload your brain in exhausting its CPU through multitasking, because the former can be remedied with some rest and extra time, while the latter can cause damage to your neural circuits and condition you to be less productive over time.

<u>TASK</u>: Write down each thing you need to do—make a list. Then run through the list categorizing what's "most urgent" to "least urgent." This will help you prioritize what you need to get done first. Then do what needs to be done first; and when you finish that task, move on to the next one. You will be able to accomplish more by working in such systematic fashion; you will have enhanced your powers of concentration. You will not be nearly as susceptible to all the "Squirrel" moments and distracting notifications that can randomly pop up out of nowhere.

MISTAKE #7:
Zombified Day State of Mind

We need sleep. We need enough sleep. We need it regularly, daily. Sleep deprivation wreaks havoc with many of the chemicals in the brain (neurotransmitters) that we need in order to be able to think clearly, to stay awake, and to make good decisions. Otherwise, we become day zombies.

REASONS: According to the Harvard University Medical School newsletter (www.health.harvard.edu/newsletter_article/sleep-and-mental-health), "Sleep problems may increase risk for developing particular mental illnesses," particularly depressive disorder.

Lots of stuff we eat and drink can keep us from falling asleep when we want to. Caffeine is big for that. Some folks can have a cup of coffee or an energy drink and be sound asleep within a few minutes, but most of us can't. Nicotine is another culprit that can keep us stimulated even when we are tired. How about that hot fudge sundae for a late dessert? Chocolate contains a stimulant like caffeine. And the sugar that's in the sundae can give us a sudden nice "rush," at exactly the wrong time.

Other things can keep us up: vigorous exercise just before bedtime can keep our minds from relaxing. Watching TV can be another "stimulant" of sorts—we usually think of watching video entertainment as essentially a "sensory deprivation" experience but watching "moving pictures" before bed may get our brains revved up and keep us awake.

Scientifically, the nuts and bolts of the "neurochemistry of sleep" is wildly complex, just like the details of how the brain itself works. There is a plethora of published scientific articles on "sleep deprivation neurotransmitters." Sure, they're rather quite technical, but you might find it interesting to further read some of their abstract summaries.

<u>BENCHMARK</u>: We don't need to worship our sleep schedules. There are plenty of times we need to stay up late. But if we make a habit of sleeping less than we need, we have a hard time keeping ourselves mentally and physically on an even keel. We can find ourselves in the unenviable position of being "dead tired" but unable to sleep. This can cause us more problems.

Let's avoid developing the habit of staying up more and sleeping less. We typically need 7-to-9 hours of sleep each day. This is not something to feel guilty about! We don't become more productive simply by staying up late and working on things; we become less. Each of us is different and our sleep patterns will change as we age. We need to be reasonably careful about how we live.

<u>TASK</u>: If you are routinely not getting enough sleep, here is some advice from the US National Institutes of Health (www.ninds.nih.gov/disorders/patient-caregiver-education/understanding-sleep#4):

- Set a schedule—go to bed and wake up at the same time each day.

- Exercise 20 to 30 minutes a day, but no later than a few hours before going to bed.

- Avoid caffeine and nicotine late in the day and alcoholic drinks before bed.

- Relax before bed—try a warm bath, reading, or another relaxing routine.

- Create a room for sleep—avoid bright lights and loud sounds, keep the room at a comfortable temperature, and don't watch TV or have a computer in your bedroom.

- Don't lie in bed awake. If you can't get to sleep, do something else, like reading or listening to music, until you feel tired.

- See a doctor if you have a problem sleeping or if you feel unusually tired during the day. Most sleep disorders can be treated effectively.

MISTAKE #8:
Toxic Interpersonal Dynamics

This is intriguing, nonetheless: our brains age faster when we are involved with people who are not encouraging and are not supportive but are instead, constantly critical of us. These folks tend to continually broadcast "bad vibes;" they "poison" everyone around them. We all know folks like that. They are just plain grumpy and can never say anything good, particularly about those nearby. They are truly a pain to be around. Some of them are close to us. Some we have to deal with daily. Some we cannot avoid.

REASONS: When we are immersed in such negativity, our brains wear out more quickly. There is an article about that entitled "Negative Aspects of Close Relationships as

Risk Factors for Cognitive Aging" (<u>American Journal of Epidemiology</u>, 1 December 2014); the conclusion for us non-epidemiological types can be found in its beginning abstract summary: "Negative aspects of close relationships, but not positive aspects, were associated with accelerated cognitive aging." In plainer speech: if we're around "toxic" people too much, we more rapidly lose our ability to think clearly.

It's easy to see, in part, why this happens. The stress of being with someone who "disapproves" of us causes a whole bunch of physiological reactions to one degree or another, mostly involving the "fight or flight" response. We remember that stress and how we felt at the time. The next time we are about to be with this "toxic" person, we anticipate the toxicity and start the stress reaction sooner. If we do this often enough, we develop patterns of thought or habits of thinking that turn us into an "Eeyore" or a "Puddleglum," always assuming the worst. We become toxic people ourselves, unable to find joy, and spoiling all of our relationships.

<u>BENCHMARK</u>: Stay away from negativity. It's easy for us to become this way, to become negative and grouchy and unable to look for the good in someone or something. Our minds tend to act like a sponge—we take to heart things said about us that are critical, whether true or not. We focus on what we are bad at, or how we have hurt somebody else. It adds unnecessary stress to the brain. We definitely don't "Keep on the Sunny Side." Learn to say "no" and move away from drama as much as you can so you can maintain a detoxified clear mind.

As another recommended read: sometimes we need a different perspective on our family and friends. Read the book <u>Irregular People</u> by Joyce Landorf Heatherley for some insights and ideas.

<u>TASK</u>: Think of three primary negative reoccurrences in your life, then possible scenarios on how to rid yourself of them; you may have to get creative. Are you frequently around someone like a family member or colleague who

berates you, doesn't encourage you, or appears to be making your life miserable? What are your options? Can you walk away (or even emigrate)? Can you resoundingly say "No!" to them? Can you consider them pitiable as people and "kill them with kindness"? Do you need professional help, like a psychologist? Would you benefit from being part of a support group? You yourself need to act, to be proactive in this. That way, you can be conscious of them and be prepared on what to do when these toxic situations emerge and protect your brain from the negative effects they have. You do not need to be the victim of a "toxic" relationship.

MISTAKE #9:
Unattended Unintended-Effects of Medical Substances

This may be a delicate subject for some, but we do need to touch on it regardless. Medication can have a profound effect on how we live. We take our medicine because we need it to either get healthy or stay healthy. But lots of drugs have an effect on how our brains work. Do we become excited, anxious, calm, or grouchy? Does a particular drug make us sleepy or does it make us incapable of falling asleep? Does it give us a tummy ache? Does it give us tremors, making it impossible for us to use our fine motor skills?

<u>REASONS</u>: Some drugs stimulate the brain: they can help keep us awake, give us more energy, make us think faster, or make us more capable of doing more for longer. Some drugs help relieve pain incredibly well; they enable us to continue to function. There are medications that ease our anxieties. There are many drugs that help us control our blood pressure or help us breathe easier. Lots and lots of good drugs for lots and lots of good reasons. But each medication we take will affect us a little differently than someone else.

Lots of "potentially mind-altering drugs" can be really helpful for treating particular conditions if used carefully and under supervision. An example of this is "Percocet," a potent pain reliever which is a combination of the "opioid oxycodone" and "Tylenol" (generic: *acetaminophen*). Another example is "Valium" (generic: *diazepam*) which is used to treat anxiety. The problem with using Percocet or Valium and many other related drugs is that these medications can be astoundingly addictive. "Addiction" (or "chemical dependence") is bad for our mental and physical health; we need to pay attention to our doctors, so we don't fall into that trap. For further reading on the subject of "drug addiction," go to the US National Institutes for Health at www.ncbi.nlm.nih.gov/books/NBK20368.

BENCHMARK: So, how do we find out what these meds are doing to us? This is where modern technology is, oh, so nice: you can find information about medications online at webmd.com and medlineplus.gov, as well as, of course, our good old friend Wikipedia.

There is also the "fine print," more commonly known as a "drug insert" that you may be given when you pick up your prescription (usually the paper is very thin, and the typeface is very small)—ask your pharmacist for it. There will be a section describing "adverse effects." This section tells you that a certain percentage of patients taking that particular medication have experienced certain undesirable "side effects." For example: a tiny fraction of patients taking "theophylline," a medication designed to help one breathe easier, can become "irritable" ("really grumpy") and can't get enough sleep.

Also be aware of the effects of the other things you take— what you routinely eat or drink as well as the non-prescription meds and supplements: if you drink a really hot cup of tea an hour before bedtime, will it keep you awake? If you have that glass of red wine with dinner, do you feel depressed the next morning? Does your antihistamine make you edgy?

TASK: Check out the medications you have been prescribed. Look them up. Pay attention to the "adverse effects" for each of these drugs. But don't become a hypochondriac and believe you are "suffering" from each of these effects as they are described; instead, dispassionately evaluate what this medication is doing to you and for you. Know why you are taking it. Talk to your doctor if you have questions, or your pharmacist. Make any changes only under the supervision of your health care provider.

MISTAKE #10:
Throwing Caution to the Wind

Our purpose with these "brain actions" is to help you identify some common habits and activities that may be holding you back: things that hinder your brain from operating at the highest level possible. Unfortunately, there's a bunch of stuff you really can't fix simply by changing your lifestyle: head trauma (that's why it's a good idea to wear a helmet while skiboarding), infections (encephalitis, for example), stroke, and various "hard-wired" mental health conditions such as bipolar disorder.

REASONS: These problems are akin to having a cracked egg, where you can't put Humpty Dumpty back together again. Some of these "conditions" actually result in the loss of brain cells. Check out: "Brain Gray Matter Deficits at 33-Year Follow-up in Adults with Attention-Deficit/Hyperactivity Disorder Established in Childhood" JAMA Psychiatry, November 2011. (Yes, this is technical, but the conclusions are stunning.)

BENCHMARK: Fret not. We are not trying to scare you into paranoia or despair. We want you to be more conscientious of the things you do. As the proverbial saying goes, "An ounce of prevention is worth a pound of cure." You always want to be safe than sorry, so practice safety measures first. Most of the time, these conditions can be prevented or managed. Sometimes we benefit from medications or dietary changes. Sometimes we need therapy of one kind or another. The good news is that the brain has an amazing ability to work around many internal abnormalities; this gives us real hope that we can overcome our own problems.

TASK: Get yourself checked out regularly, particularly if you smacked your head while falling off your bicycle (even if you were wearing a helmet). Make sure the stuff between your ears is working well. If there are other problems—ADHD, bipolar disorder, or some other mental health issue—pay attention to your doctor's recommendations. Take your meds. Do your therapy. Keep working at it! As we said before, the brain has an amazing ability to work around problems, so don't ever give up trying to get better. Miracles do happen that even science can't explain.

ENCORE ACT:
Fire Up the Synapses

TASK 1: Become a voracious reader. Read lots of different kinds of things—articles, novels, poetry, non-fiction, and so on. Find out what you like to read and get into it.

TASK 2: Write stuff down. Organize your thoughts on paper. Make lists. Keep a paper calendar. Engage your brain and your fine motor skills.

TASK 3: Exercise your brain. Use a variety of puzzles like crossword, sudoku, and word find as a start. Build things with Legos. Put together a jigsaw puzzle or three. Resist spending too much time absorbing video input.

<u>TASK 4</u>: Eat better. Part of a balanced diet is making sure you eat enough of the right kinds of fatty acids. Your entire nervous system will thank you.

<u>TASK 5</u>: Decrease your dependence on automation. This supplements TASK 2: manually organize your own life, yourself.

<u>TASK 6</u>: Do one thing at a time sequentially rather simultaneously. You will be able to concentrate better, and you'll get more done.

<u>TASK 7</u>: Get enough sleep. You need it. Here's an analogy: the next time you fly somewhere, listen to the flight attendant's briefing about the oxygen masks (we should listen anyway). You are instructed to put on the oxygen mask first before helping anyone else. The reason? You can't help anyone, including yourself, if you lose consciousness because you are deprived of oxygen. In the same way, your life will be much more difficult, and your

brain will not work very well, if you deprive yourself of the sleep you need.

TASK 8: Either transform or get rid of all your "toxic" relationships. Your brain will love you for it because negativity decreases its mental power like Kryptonite.

TASK 9: Know what your medications are doing to you. Be in communication with your health care providers. Learn how you, yourself, respond to any particular thing you are taking. Keep track of what you are taking and when and if you seem to have any problems after starting a new med (write it down, keep a journal).

TASK 10: Practice safety first. If you do have any form of disability, keep at it; never give up. Regardless of what you have on your plate, strive to do as well as you can. Never quit trying.

F(ULL) ACE AT REVEAL:
Neural Circuitry Rewired

As we said from the very beginning, our brains tend to wear out as we get older. Unfortunately, some of us wear out sooner than we should. None of us can predict our own futures.

Fortunately, there are ways of working to get the best out of our "gray matter" for as long as possible. We can support flexing our neuroplasticity, maintaining our mental sharpness, and diminishing the onslaught of mental disorders later in life like dementia and Alzheimer's disease.

It has been said: "Live fast, die young, and leave a good-looking corpse." Not a good idea. It's better to read more, write more, and eat the nutritious foods that help our brains and bodies work as efficiently as they can. We can harness these everyday life skills so we can continue to communicate clearly (it's a good idea to be able to keep using our words), and maybe even be able to answer our emails.

And do get enough rest—remember we are trying to avoid wearing ourselves out. We get to share the love for a lot longer. (We might even remember the names of our grandchildren, and how to read to them, as well as teach them a thing or two with how Grandpa/Grandma used to have done things back in the good old days.)

Don't let life pass you by. Work to maintain the memories of what matter most to you. Work to preserve your self-sufficiency, your quality of life. Do what you can do to take care of your brain so that you can use it longer. Because after all—a beautiful mind is, indeed, a terrible thing to waste.